IMAGES
of America

PENN STATE BLUE BAND

On the Cover: There were many musical organizations at Penn State when it was known as the Pennsylvania Farmer's High School. One of the first was the Fife and Bugle Corps. The corps would start, disband, and restart multiple times in the 1870s and 1880s but had ceased to operate by the 1890s. This left a void that was filled by the Cadet Band, the group that eventually became the Blue Band. (Courtesy of the Pennsylvania State University Photograph Collection.)

IMAGES
of America

PENN STATE BLUE BAND

Thomas E. Range II and Lewis Lazarow

ISBN 978-1-4671-0634-4

Published by Arcadia Publishing
Charleston, South Carolina

Printed in the United States of America

Library of Congress Control Number: 2020949264

For all general information, please contact Arcadia Publishing:
Telephone 843-853-2070
Fax 843-853-0044
E-mail sales@arcadiapublishing.com
For customer service and orders:
Toll-Free 1-888-313-2665

Visit us on the Internet at www.arcadiapublishing.com

In memory of our friend April Strong,
and in honor of the 2020 Blue Band—the love of
music unites us across the generations.

Contents

ACKNOWLEDGMENTS

There are many people to acknowledge for the creation of this book. First and foremost are our families. Maureen, Sharon, Megan, Jake, Anya, and Mitchell provided the love and support to make this book possible.

Secondly, numerous Blue Band alumni and former staff members responded to our questions, providing in-depth information and images. To name just a few: Karen Walk, Jim Lawrence, Mark Poblete, Dean DeVore, Dick Bundy, Kathy Bamet, Lori Uhazie, Sue Delanko, Amy Litwiler, Brad Townsend, Dave Paden, Steven Stept, and Jake Lazarow.

The current Blue Band staff should be commended for their support of this book as well as the support they give to the many students who are currently in the band: Dr. Gregory Drane, Robert Hickey Jr., Wanda Hockenberry, Dave Buzminsky, Charlie Robey, Heather Bean, Matt Freeman, Kris Kimmel, David Cree, Kent Martin, and Annmarie Mountz.

Lastly, we must thank the Pennsylvania State University Archives for many of the photographs used in this volume. Though purchased and now in the authors' personal collection for more than 20 years, the Pennsylvania State University Archives deserves credit for preserving the history of Penn State. Images purchased from the archives will be denoted as from the Pennsylvania State University Photograph Collection (FTPSUPC) throughout this book.

INTRODUCTION

The Penn State Blue Band is one of the most respected marching bands in the country. What started as a small cadet band of six male members has grown to a group of about 325 dedicated young men and women, who work together each season to represent their university; entertain fans, family, friends, fellow students, and alumni; and honor the legacy of excellence established across 120 years.

Penn State started as an agricultural high school but had military roots. Following military tradition, musical units were used to give commands and cadences. The precursor of the Blue Band, the Cadet Band, was strictly military in nature. As the band grew, a professional director was hired, Wilfred Otto "Tommy" Thompson. A former military man himself, he would continue the military-influenced traditions of the band. It was under his direction, however, that part of the band played for football games, and when the school purchased a limited number of blue uniforms that differed from the band's traditional khaki ones, he was the one who coined the name "Blue Band" in 1923. The Blue Band subset of the College Military Band (as the Cadet Band was renamed during World War I) played at football games at home and away.

When Hummel Fishburn was hired to replace the retiring Thompson, he changed the direction of the Blue Band into more of a collegiate style of performance. The band started to perform halftime shows and form images and words on the field. The membership continued to be all male except during World War II when women were allowed into the band. After the war, a coed Concert Blue Band was created, while the Marching Blue Band returned to all-male membership. Due to his many responsibilities as director of both the music department and music education department, Fishburn decided to hire James Dunlop to take over the Blue Band responsibilities.

The band continued to grow and evolve under Dunlop; he was responsible for starting such traditions as Band Day and the Alumni Band and supporting the establishment of the Touch of Blue majorettes as well as the silk line. His tenure saw the origination of the drum major flip and the full integration of women instrumentalists. Marching in the Blue Band at the time was a young O. Richard Bundy. Dunlop was key in hiring assistant director Ned Deihl, who continued Dunlop's vision of innovation; as assistant director, he created the Blue Band's trademark pregame drill, the Floating Lions.

Deihl became director of the Blue Band when Dunlop unexpectedly passed away in 1975. Deihl continued to grow the band and started his own tradition of Bandorama, with the Blue Band performing its halftime music year-in-review in a concert setting. At this point, Penn State football was really taking off, and Beaver Stadium was undergoing major expansion projects, which prompted Deihl to expand the band membership so spectators could better see what the band was doing. Deihl hired O. Richard Bundy as assistant director; together, the two oversaw the Blue Band program and in 1993 Penn State became the 11th member of the Big Ten—a conference steeped in tradition, notable for fielding some of the oldest and greatest marching bands in the nation. The Blue Band felt right at home amid such company.

In 1996, Dr. Deihl retired and passed the directorship to Dr. Bundy. Under Bundy's direction, the Blue Band accomplished things that would have been unimaginable even 25 years before: the construction of the Blue Band Building in 2004, at long last giving the band a permanent home—one that would ultimately bear Bundy's name; receiving the Sudler Trophy, the greatest honor possible in the world of collegiate marching bands, in 2005—mere months before appearing on the catwalk at the Marc Jacobs fashion show in New York and again in a *Vogue* photograph shoot with Kiera Knightley; and witnessing the Mid-Atlantic Emmy-winning success of *Making the Blue Band*, a Penn State Public Broadcasting documentary that chronicled the hopes of eight aspiring auditioners vying to join the band. Through it all, membership continued to expand, so to accommodate the additional performers, he tweaked the pregame show, doubling the lines of the "S."

With the retirement of Bundy in 2015, directorship of the band passed to Gregory Drane, who was a graduate assistant and then assistant director of the Blue Band under Bundy. Drane has a flair for innovative halftime shows, often making creative use of Beaver Stadium's upgraded multimedia capabilities. Under his direction, the band has continued to grow. In 2020, Drane still held auditions for the Blue Band, in the hopes that the band would perform. Unfortunately, due to Covid-19, no spectators were allowed at any of the football games, including the band. The band did hold a virtual performance for parents, friends, and fans. The band also ran a performance in an empty Beaver Stadium, which was recorded for use during the televised football games.

For over 120 years, the Blue Band has pursued and achieved excellence. It has represented Penn State, and the commonwealth of Pennsylvania, with honor. Since 1959, the Blue Band has traveled to support the Nittany Lions at 47 bowl games, including all five major bowls: the Rose, Orange, Sugar, Fiesta, and Cotton Bowls. It traveled to Philadelphia to play in the Bicentennial Constitution Celebration Parade in 1987 and to Indianapolis for the team's first appearance in the Big Ten conference championship game in 2016. The band has provided the music for the Pennsylvania governor's inauguration ceremony in Harrisburg and "shuffled off to Buffalo" four times as the featured halftime performance for the National Football League's Buffalo Bills.

But perhaps more valuable than the challenge of music and marching, more exhilarating than the travel, the shows, and the cheering crowds, are the lessons learned. The Blue Band succeeds because its students take pride in every step and every note, conscious of the weight of history and the watchful eyes of generations of alumni. The Blue Band excels because the students who arrive as rookies grow to become strong leaders, on and off the field. The Blue Band legacy endures because what starts out as friendships made during those few short college years becomes nothing less than a family of thousands who all know what it means to have donned that blue and white uniform, to raise the song for the glory of Old State.

One

From Humble Beginnings to a Military Band

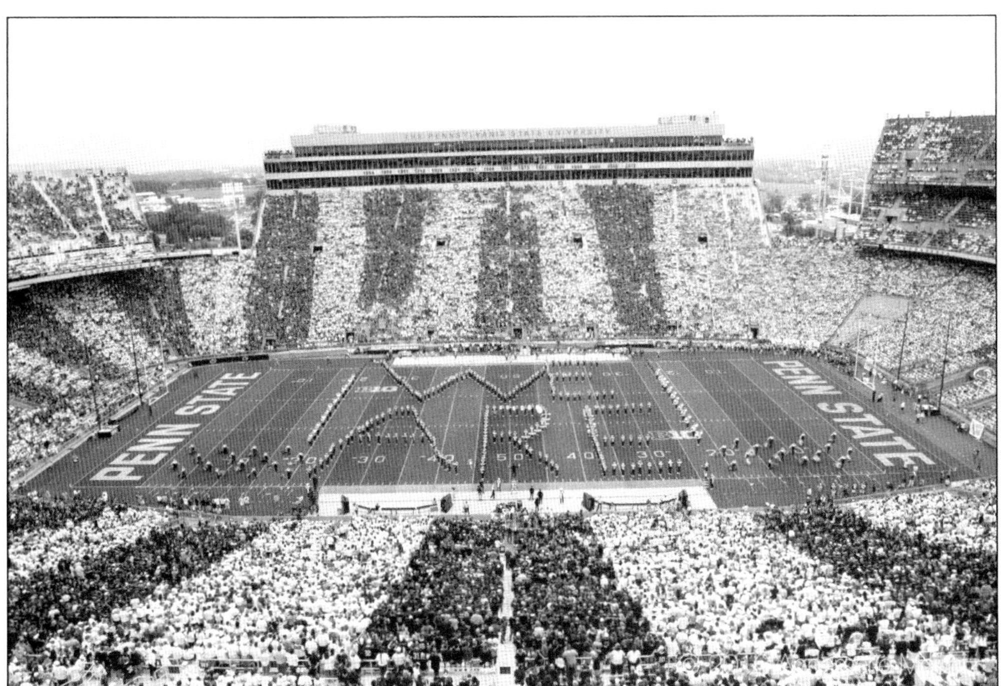

The Penn State Blue Band has a long and storied history. Now boasting about 325 members, including instrumentalists, silks, majorettes, a feature twirler, and a drum major, the band traces its origins back over 120 years to a group of six students. This is the story, told through photographs, of one of the most renowned and prestigious college marching bands in the country. (Courtesy of Annmarie Mountz.)

One day when Penn State's commandant of cadets Capt. Thomas Taliaferro was inspecting the dormitories, he noticed a bugle hanging on a wall. It belonged to George Deike, who had served during the Spanish-American War. Taliaferro charged Deike with creating a musical group, and in 1899, the Cadet Band was born. Pictured are, from left to right, (seated) George Deike and Percy Snoeberger; (standing) John Craig, George Washington Dodge, Edgar Godard, and Edwin Norris. (FTPSUPC.)

The Cadet Band quickly grew. One obstacle that the band faced was that not all the musicians owned instruments. When told of this plight, the great steel magnate Andrew Carnegie donated $800 to the band with the following note: "I have long held that there is no better way for a boy to get the devilment out of his system than to blow it out through a brass horn." (FTPSUPC.)

By the early 1900s, the band was adding new members every year. Although the administration supported the band with instruments and uniforms, the group was student-led. Some years there was a drum major as well as a president/student leader, but no official faculty director or professional conductor led the band. The band is seen here standing in front of Schwab Auditorium, which had just been completed in 1903. (FTPSUPC.)

One of the last student conductors was Capt. W.A. Moyer, pictured here in front of the 1912 Cadet Band. Note that the uniforms are slightly different with the addition of a cord, and the bass drum head has changed. There would only be one other student director after Moyer, George Sumner in 1913. The band is seated in concert formation in front of Schwab Auditorium. (FTPSUPC.)

By 1914, the band had grown to the point that it needed a professional director. Penn State president Edwin Sparks hired Wilfred Otto "Tommy" Thompson as bandmaster. Sparks had marched with and served as student president of the Ohio State Marching Band. Thompson maintained the tradition of spring concerts, even allowing some string instruments to play—note the cello at center. (FTPSUPC.)

In 1918, the band officially changed its name from the Cadet Band to the College Military Band. It continued to play both indoor and outdoor concerts. In this photograph, the 1920 College Military Band performs in front of the obelisk under Thompson's direction. Built along the mall in 1896, the 33-foot-tall obelisk remains a prominent campus landmark today. (FTPSUPC.)

During the 1920s and 1930s, the College Military Band continued to grow. As an official musical group of the college, it was called on to perform at different campus venues for various events—football games, of course, but also parades and graduation ceremonies, as shown here. The ceremony would be preceded by a procession of graduating students, faculty, and administrators, which the band would lead. (FTPSUPC.)

Following the graduation procession, the band (pictured at lower left) took its place to provide music during the ceremony. The graduating class was seated on long benches in the middle; friends and family gathered in a ring around the outside to watch. (FTPSUPC.)

The standard College Military Band uniforms were brown, in keeping with military tradition; the US Army had established khaki as the color of the service uniform since 1902. But in 1923, the college purchased a number of new blue uniforms—however, there were not enough of them for all band members. Thompson made the decision that the band's top players would earn the right to wear the new blue uniforms, while everyone else continued to wear the old brown ones. Officially the unit was still known as the College Military Band, but this smaller group of top players began to be referred to as the Blue Band. They were the band that played at home football games at New Beaver Field and also traveled to away games. These dark blue uniforms can be seen here in the eight ranks at the center; Thompson is standing in front. (FTPSUPC.)

The Blue Band traveled to away games, like this one against the University of Pennsylvania at storied Franklin Field in 1924. Here, the band is performing on the field as the cheerleaders prepare a cheer. Incredibly, the band was witness to the game ending in a 0-0 tie—an extraordinary defensive effort by the Lions, as that season the Penn Quakers outscored their opponents 203-31. (FTPSUPC.)

By 1927, the Blue Band was firmly established as the premier marching band at Penn State College. In this image, the Blue Band is in rank formation along with the rest of the College Military Band. The Blue Band members in their blue uniforms form a letter "S" within the block. (FTPSUPC.)

The 1938–1939 school year marked the last year the Blue Band was under the leadership of Tommy Thompson (first row, center). When he retired at the end of the season, the band presented him with a gold pocket watch that had the letters of his name in place of numbers, over the Penn State seal. His parting words to the band were: "I'm 103 years old, but I can still make more noise on a trumpet than the whole damn bunch of you!" The Thompson pocket watch was donated back to the band in 2004 by his grandson Ted Thompson and is now on display in the lobby of the O. Richard Bundy Blue Band Building (ORBBBB). In 2015, the Blue Band gave Bundy an exact replica of this historic watch in honor of his own retirement as director. (FTPSUPC.)

In 1939, Penn State elevated Hum Fishburn to replace Thompson as the leader of the Blue Band (first row, center). Fishburn was a Penn State alumnus, having earned both his bachelor of arts (1922) and master of arts (1925) there. He had been a professor at the college since 1928, directing the Symphony Orchestra, Women's Chorus, Men's Glee Club, and the Women's Symphony Orchestra. He created the music appreciation class at Penn State and wrote the textbook *Fundamentals of Music Appreciation* for it. In 1942, Fishburn became the chair of both the music and music education programs within the School of Liberal Arts, and oversaw the entire department's move from Schwab Auditorium to the former Carnegie Library building, renamed Carnegie Hall. He was also personally responsible for producing *OPUS*, the official newsletter of the Department of Music—a task he handled for all 23 years of his time as chair. (FTPSUPC.)

For the 1943 season, the Blue Band performed only limited field drills on the field. With so many men called to active duty, the Blue Band could no longer be an all-male group and still perform. Thus, for the first time in the band's history, women became members and would continue to be an important part of the band until 1946, when the men returned from the war. However, because there were women who still wanted to perform, the Concert Blue Band was created to accommodate both male and female performers, while the Marching Blue Band returned to all-male membership to perform at football games. In 1947, Hum Fishburn hired Dr. James Dunlop to take over the Blue Band responsibilities. Dunlop is pictured here conducting the 1947 Concert Blue Band during an outdoor performance; the band is mostly male with some female instrumentalists. (Courtesy of Edith Murray.)

After the war, the Blue Band returned to its standard shows of creating words or letters on the field, but it would take a few years for the wartime decline in membership to reverse. To carry out more intricate field show performances, membership had to grow. (FTPSUPC.)

By 1948, membership in the Blue Band reached 100. Here, the band is in a postgame block formation on New Beaver Field, with drum major Jay Lucas front and center and Dunlop to the right. To the left is probably Hum Fishburn, who continued to write shows as well as announce for the band. (FTPSUPC.)

The Blue Band's drum major wears a different uniform so he is easily identified. The military-style jacket is accompanied by the tall, traditional busby hat. He carries a mace—a long baton with a round top—originally used to signal parade commands to the band. Today, drum majors use a whistle to give commands and establish musical tempos; twirling and tossing the mace is now part of their performance. (FTPSUPC.)

The Blue Band has long had a saying: "If you're early, you're on time. If you're on time, you're late. If you're late, you're out." Keeping one's block spot means arriving at practices early and being ready to play when the whistle blows. Arriving late might mean a band member watches that week's performance from the sidelines. Band members do what must be done to get to practice on time. (FTPSUPC.)

By 1949, membership had grown sufficiently to allow the band to spell out the letters "PSC" (for Penn State College) instead of just an "S." That same year, New Beaver Field received its final seating upgrade; at capacity, the Blue Band now performed in front of a crowd of 27,720 for every home game. (FTPSUPC.)

One of Dunlop's innovations was to invite area high school bands to come to a football game and perform with the Blue Band. Band Day, as it was called, helped advertise the Blue Band to potential future members and gave spectators at New Beaver Field a stunning sight when the bands combined to create the "PSC" formation. (FTPSUPC.)

Throughout its entire early history, including in this image from the 1950s, the Blue Band marched the "6 to 5" stride that was the standard for military-style marching bands. This means it took six steps to cover a distance of five yards. At 30 inches per step, each band member's stride was much longer than a normal walking gait, which made it appropriate for parades as well as field shows that mostly consisted of block movements and countermarching. Years later, as collegiate bands shifted away from military style, the standard evolved into "8 to 5," a 22.5-inch stride that remains the most popular choice among school bands today. Based on the fact that fans are still arriving at New Beaver Field and the Blue Band is marching out of the end zone, this image shows the start of a pregame show. (FTPSUPC.)

In 1953, Penn State had grown to the point where it finally achieved recognition as a university. While he was glad to have accomplished this goal, university president Milton Eisenhower was concerned about the confusion it might cause to have the now university's mailing address located in the town of State College. He then launched a new campaign: getting the campus to have its own post office and zip code. With a little help from his brother, US president Dwight D. Eisenhower, the separate entity called University Park came into existence, with the zip code 16802. Of course, for the Blue Band, the school's change in status required a formation adjustment; the traditional Band Day event at New Beaver Field replaced the large "PSC" with a "PSU." Note that on the track surrounding the field, the female front members of each of the high school bands on the field—flag, rifle, and majorette squads—are facing the crowd and arrayed to perform. (FTPSUPC.)

Two

Becoming a College Band

Hum Fishburn retired in 1965 as professor emeritus, and the band paid tribute to him on the field. Over his 37 years of service to the school, he was the architect of monumental changes to the Blue Band. Even in retirement, his association with the Blue Band did not end. He continued to serve as the Blue Band announcer up until his death in 1976. (FTPSUPC.)

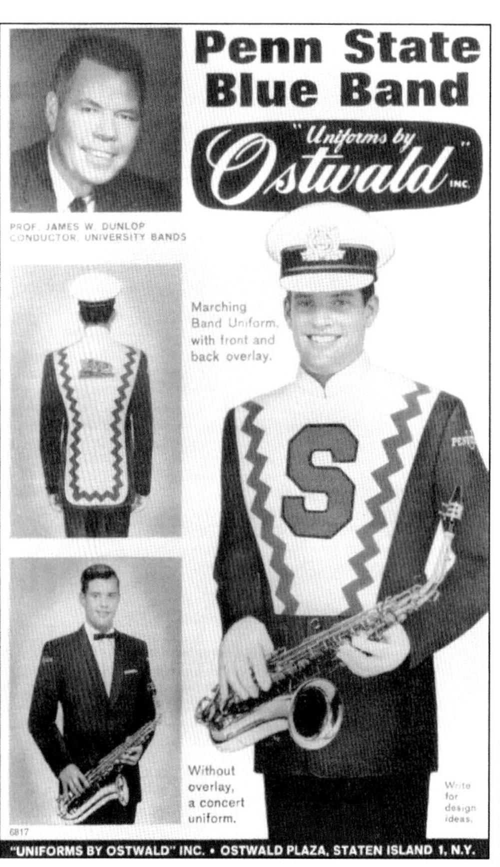

Dunlop embraced and continued Fishburn's evolution of the Blue Band, instituting a drastic change in uniform in 1963. Previously the band would be dressed in more of a military style, but Dunlop reached out to Ostwald Inc. to create an appearance more befitting a collegiate band. The new style incorporated a suit jacket and trousers for the concert band performances, with a white plastic overlay worn on top of the jacket for marching band. The performers provided their own black dress shoes, and those in the marching band also received spats to cover them to create uniformity. Having a dual-purpose uniform was certainly cost-saving; however, those marching in the Blue Band essentially did so in a wool suit. (Both, FTPSUPC.)

The year 1963 also marked the creation of the Alumni Band. Over the 18 years Dunlop served as Blue Band director, he had stayed in touch with many of his former students, and invited them to come join the Blue Band for a game. They would be allowed to sit in the stands with the student members of the Blue Band and get back on the field to perform a show. In order to make this annual reunion possible, Dunlop relied upon the assistance of Blue Band alumni Dick Ammon, Rich Victor, John Kovolchik, and John Prendergast, who were all still living in the State College area; in fact, Victor and Kovolchik were State College music teachers. This new Blue Band tradition came at the perfect time, as the Nittany Lions were still making themselves at home in their new "den"—Beaver Stadium, which had been completed in 1960. The Blue Band now performed in front of a home crowd of 46,284 Penn State fans. (FTPSUPC.)

The Alumni Blue Band Association grew over the years to boast more than 1,000 members, all of whom look forward to the opportunity to return to campus and perform on the field once again. One of the traditional highlights is the combined Blue Band and Alumni Blue Band performance. In the image above, the Alumni Blue Band members, wearing white tops and dark pants, form "PENN," while current students of the Blue Band, dressed in the traditional uniform, stand alongside them forming "STATE." Below, the alumni form the "S" of the "PSU" formation. The performance would traditionally end with the "Singing Lion," with band members young and old singing the first verse together, then playing the second. (Both, FTPSUPC.)

Another Blue Band tradition began in 1965 when assistant director Ned C. Deihl created the Floating Lions drill. Deihl wanted the band to explode out of the stadium tunnel, which was at the time in the north end zone, then form the word "LIONS" and float it across the field as if it were on an electronic sign in Times Square. Eventually, he would add to the drill by having the formation flip and float back the other way, so that "LIONS" could be read by fans sitting on the east side of the stadium as well. By the mid-1970s, the Beaver Stadium expansion project closed off the north end zone and relocated the tunnel under the new permanent south stands; the drill was changed to accommodate the new entrance and established a pregame show that the band still performs. (Both, FTPSUPC.)

Before the origination of the now traditional "Drum Major Flip" by Jeff Robertson in 1971, the Blue Band drum major could choose to do anything he wanted. Most were either acrobatic or could handle or twirl a mace rather well. The 1960s also saw the creation of a flag corps within the band that eventually became known as the silks. The original silks were alternates in the band, holding extra-large flags during the procession down the field. These flags were a lot larger than the current ones used by the silk squad, preventing the users from doing any routines. The band was still completely male at this time. (Both, FTPSUPC.)

In the fall of 1965, a young Orrin Richard "Dick" Bundy Jr. joined the Blue Band as a trombonist. He is one of the trombonists in this promotional image from 1968 showcasing drum major Stanley "Chip" Willis. Note Willis's uniform: the style of wearing flared-hip riding breeches and tall boots originated from equestrian sportsmen and cavalry officers, then came to be strongly associated as a way to present oneself as a figure of authority. This is also reflected in the presence of the white fringed shoulder epaulets (difficult to see against the sky), and the sleeve braid, which is done in the pattern of a US Army first lieutenant during the Civil War. The triple braid and feather plume are still on the drum major's busby hat today. This was the final version of the drum major's overlay to have "PSU" on the front. To match the full band's uniform change in the early 1970s, the drum major also adopted the overlapping "PS" logo. (FTPSUPC.)

In 1971, Jeff Robertson created a tradition that has since become a legendary part of Penn State Blue Band and football history. Being a gymnast and not much of a baton/mace twirler, Robertson decided to add a flip into the drum major's routine for pregame—but chose not to tell Dunlop about it. When he got off the field, Dunlop went up to him and asked, "Do you plan to do that every game?" Robertson said, "Yes," to which Dunlop replied, "Don't screw it up!" The original flip was a back flip, but drum major Ron Louder changed it to a front flip in 1977. Landing the flip is now a mandatory element of the Blue Band drum major's responsibility; legend says that if the drum major makes the flip, Penn State will win the game. (FTPSUPC.)

The year 1971 also saw a significant change in the uniform overlay. The new version removed the lightning bolts around the edges, and the words "Nittany Lions" replaced the image of the Nittany Lion Shrine on the back. The front of the overlay had a "PS" instead of just an "S," and tassels were added on the shoulders. The suit jacket and trousers, however, remained the same—and just as uncomfortable and hot to march in. That problem would not be solved until the next complete uniform redesign in 2008. (Right, FTPSUPC; below, courtesy of Thomas Range II.)

These two images of sousaphone players during pregame are from the 1970s and 1980s respectively; they look nearly identical except for one tiny uniform detail. The new overlays received in 1971 had a white stripe around the collar. A few years later, another shipment of new overlays arrived, but these did not have that white stripe. As a result, the Blue Band managers at the time had to go through every older overlay and tear the stripes off the collars so they would match. That collar stripe is also visible in the early silk squad photograph on the facing page. (Both, FTPSUPC.)

In 1972, student Judy Shearer met with Dunlop in hopes of joining the band as a majorette. The band had been all male since World War II and had never fielded a majorette line. Shearer's audition impressed Dunlop; he charged her with finding additional twirlers for a squad. Shearer found 60 candidates, from whom she and Dunlop selected a squad of 12. Shearer is in the first row at far left. (FTPSUPC.)

As this image of the silk squad from the early 1970s shows, the poles are much shorter than they were in the previous decade, which allowed the members to perform routines. Most of the squad members are male and wearing the same uniform as the instrumentalists in the band. In contrast, the Blue Band silk squads today are mostly female and wear a completely different uniform than the instrumentalists. (FTPSUPC.)

This image shows the band in the mid- to late 1970s. It has grown into a 12-by-12 block of performers. Majorettes can be seen along the goal line in the upper left. The silk squad is still wearing the same uniforms as the instrumentalists. The chief difference here is the presence of the feature twirler, front and center, beside the drum major. That position was not created until 1974, when Dunlop chose Lori Donaldson to be the first feature twirler. She wore a different uniform than the rest of the majorettes. However, the first official title for the feature twirler, Star Sapphire, was not used until 1978. It was then changed to Blue Sapphire, the title still given to the Blue Band female feature twirlers today. (FTPSUPC.)

When the tunnel entrance in Beaver Stadium was in the north end zone during the 1960s, the band ranks were arranged so that the first two ranks of trombones would lead the band out for the pregame show. When the tunnel was moved to the south after the stadium expansion in the mid-1970s, the drill was flipped, resulting in the clarinet and piccolo ranks leading the band out. (Courtesy of Thomas Range II.)

The 1989 Blue Band staff was faced with an unenviable task—choosing between two extraordinary students for the coveted position of Blue Band feature twirler. In the end, the staff could not justify making a choice, so both John Mitchell and Lori Branley were named feature twirlers for the 1989, 1990, and 1991 seasons. Mitchell stayed on for one more season as the lone feature twirler in 1992. (FTPSUPC.)

During the pregame show, the opening piece is a version of the "Nittany Lion," a traditional Penn State school song since the early 1920s when it was composed by student James Leyden. The Blue Band's accompanying drill is divided into three sections. Once all instrumentalists, silks, and majorettes have emerged from the tunnel and are in place in block formation in the end zone, the band plays the 28-beat "Hail to the Lion" fanfare. In the eight beats between the end of the fanfare and the start of the downfield march, the announcer introduces the drum major, who is already on the run out from the middle of the block. As he approaches the 50-yard line, the Beaver Stadium crowd collectively holds its breath as he jumps up and completes his traditional front flip. Landing it, the stadium roars its approval, and the drum major drops into a split and salutes the west-side stands. (FTPSUPC.)

The trained eye can understand a lot from this image of the Blue Band at practice. First, based on the condition of the practice field, it is later in the season; months of marching have entirely worn away the grass at the center of the field and left a grid of dirt trenches across the rest. A director is standing atop the scaffolding in front of the two trailers used for instrument storage along the sideline—the Brake Blue Band Tower and the Blue Band Building are both years in the future. The band is taking the field from the back sideline instead of the end zone, signifying that they are practicing a halftime show, not pregame. Finally, the particular style of Blue Band jacket seen here was made and worn by band members from 1989 through the mid-1990s. (Courtesy of Lewis Lazarow.)

Penn State played in the Kickoff Classic against Georgia Tech at the Meadowlands on August 28, 1991. The Blue Band and the Yellow Jacket Marching Band provided a combined performance of the national anthem. This explains why the Blue Band's "PSU" monogram formation is centered on the 20-yard line instead of the 50; the Yellow Jackets are about to take their positions on the other half of the field. (Courtesy of Lewis Lazarow.)

Here, the Blue Band is practicing the pregame Floating Lions drill. The snare drummers, forming the top of the upright of the "N" in "LIONS," have all hit the yard line at the same time. The sousaphones, however, are forming the diagonal of the "N." In order to create this effect, they march at one-step intervals behind each other and as a result would hit one beat after each other. (Courtesy of Jennifer Greenfield Attock.)

Of the three Blockbuster Bowls held in the early 1990s, Penn State played in two of them—and so did the Blue Band. At the very end of the halftime show during the third Blockbuster Bowl in 1992, the band is in what is known as a company front. The instrumentalists are all shoulder-to-shoulder at a one-step interval along the front sideline, stretching across the entire length of the field from end zone to end zone. With over 200 instrumentalists, it is easy to double that line, with the back line standing while the front line kneels. The result is visually impressive, but the wall of sound directed up into the faces of everyone sitting in and below the press box is perhaps most impressive. In the foreground, note the drum major's mace; the drum major himself, Tom Roberts, is on a ladder out of frame as one of the conductors for the finale. (Courtesy of Lewis Lazarow.)

This view of the start of pregame from a student's perspective shows the block band forming from the tunnel entrance. Some of the ranks of the block have already formed while others are just starting. The first rank on the field is the drum line, which comes out to the 10-yard line to start the cadence; they will actually be in the middle of the block band once it is fully formed. (Courtesy of Sharon Lazarow.)

Pictured is a group photograph of the 275 members of the 1992 Blue Band. At bottom left are Dr. O. Richard Bundy and Dr. Ned C. Deihl. Centered at the bottom are feature twirler John Mitchell and drum major Tom Roberts. In only 25 years, the band had doubled in size. (Courtesy of the Blue Band Office.)

Three

JOINING THE NATIONAL COLLEGIATE ELITE

Penn State played its first football game as a member of the Big Ten Conference on September 4, 1993, winning the home opener against the University of Minnesota. In commemoration of this historic occasion, the Blue Band recreated the new Big Ten logo as part of its halftime show—the number "11" straddles either side of the "T," signifying Penn State was the 11th member added to the conference. (Courtesy of Lewis Lazarow.)

Part of the technical complexity of the Blue Band's pregame show comes as a result of how the show is designed: each instrumentalist in the block has a unique set of marching moves. Thus, each member becomes the expert for his or her spot. In this photograph from a rehearsal of the pregame drill, trumpeter Erin Eck has just passed sousaphonist Dave Arnoldi. Only a couple years after this photograph was taken, they were married. A few years after that they had a daughter, Brenna Arnoldi, who would grow up to play mellophone in the Blue Band from 2017 to 2020. This is not an isolated occurrence; countless students have met their significant others during their time together in Blue Band and have made marching for Penn State a family tradition. (Courtesy of Jennifer Greenfield Attock.)

The Blue Band has always depended on donations for financial support, without which the upkeep of such things as instruments and uniforms would be impossible. As a token of appreciation to donors who provided funds for replacement uniforms, the 1994 Blue Band posed for this postcard, which was sent to anyone who gave a donation. (Courtesy of the Blue Band Office.)

The year 1999 marked the 100th anniversary of the Penn State Blue Band, an occasion that called for something special for the combined student/alumni halftime show at homecoming. The result was the "100" formation—the Blue Band forming the numbers, surrounded by hundreds of alumni instrumentalists, silks, majorettes, feature twirlers, and drum majors representing decades of shared history and tradition. (Courtesy of Jim Lawrence.)

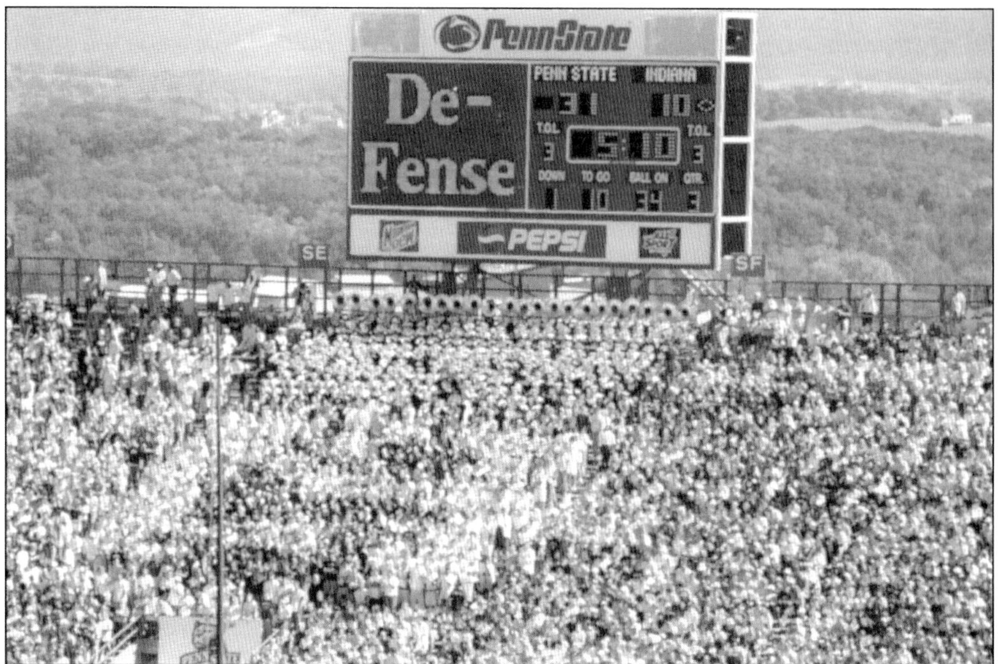

The Blue Band sat in many different areas of Beaver Stadium throughout its history. One of the best places the band ever had was under the south end scoreboard. The advantages were many: a great view of the game, no spectators behind yelling at the sousaphones to put their bells down, and in the days before there was a net to catch the ball after a field goal or extra point, band members were responsible for sending the football over the railing into the parking lot below. When the south end zone upper deck was completed in 2001, the band had to be moved because any music played beneath the overhang reverberated back at them. (Both, courtesy of the Blue Band Office.)

As the Blue Band grew in size, the pregame drill had to be changed to accommodate more performers. The first change was in the late 1980s, when there was an abundance of sousaphone players. A new rank was added to the middle of the band, called "S" rank, composed of sousaphone players as well as other instrumentalists; this later addition explains why "S" is the only rank that is not in alphabetical order. The band grew even larger in the 2000s, making a much more noticeable change in the "PSU" formation. In the new formation, the top, bottom, and sides of the "S" are now doubled. (Both, courtesy of the Blue Band Office.)

The Alumni Blue Band does not only perform at homecoming. Alumni Pep Bands have played for Philadelphia Flyers, 76ers, and Phillies games, among other gigs. The Alumni Band has even been asked to provide a pep band when the Blue Band is unavailable and often fields requests from Alumni Association chapters. (Courtesy of Thomas Range II.)

When the band performs the alma mater during the pregame show, it turns to face different sides of the stadium with each verse. During the second verse, the band faces the east sideline, and the fans on the west see a significantly brighter "PSU" formation when the sun reflects directly off the white overlays. (Courtesy of the Blue Band Office.)

The "PSU" formation is not the only change the pregame drill has seen as a result of the band's increased size. In the Floating Lions drill, the bottom of the "L"; the top and bottom of the "O"; and the top, middle, and bottom of the "S" in "LIONS" are all now doubled to accommodate more performers. (Courtesy of the Blue Band Office.)

In an effort to create more consistent and coordinated fundraising for the Blue Band and other Penn State band programs, the Floating Lions Club was established in 2000. The main goals of the organization are to provide financial support for the care and replacement of instruments, the hiring of graduate assistants, and the composition of original musical arrangements. (Courtesy of the Blue Band Office.)

Kathy Smith Bamet, silk instructor, poses with the 2000 silk line. The 2000 line went with a more military-looking uniform. The band front, consisting of the silks and majorette lines, can change uniforms each season and sometimes during a game. (Courtesy of Kathy Bamet.)

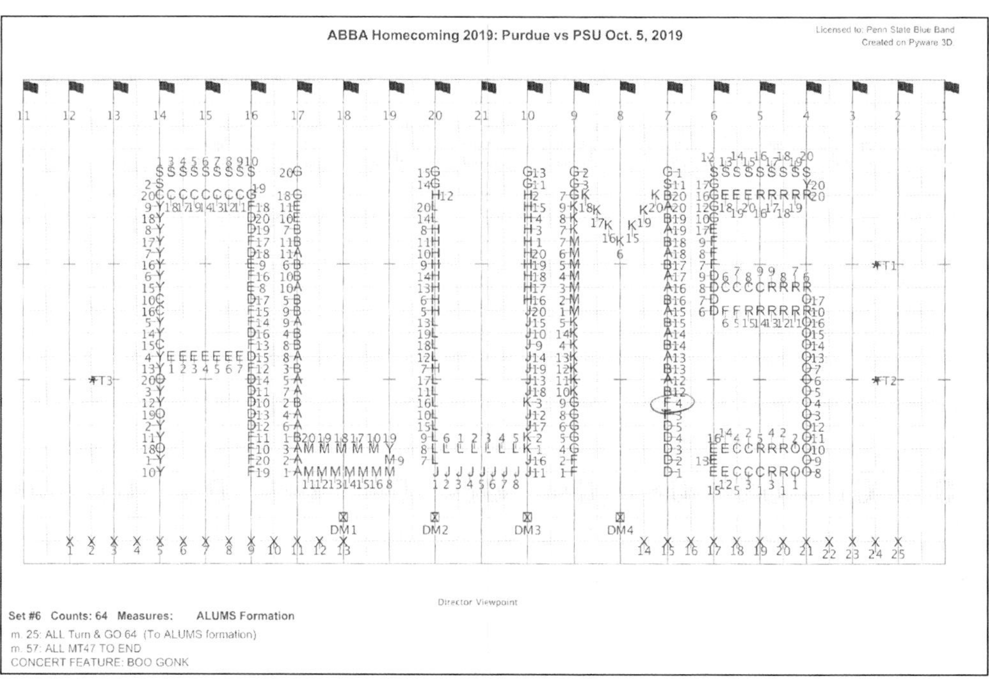

One of the greatest things a Blue Band alumnus looks forward to after graduating is returning to perform at homecoming. Every year, hundreds of Alumni Blue Band members take part in the annual homecoming traditions, particularly getting back on the Beaver Stadium field to march once again. The Alumni Blue Band members are given charts and learn the drill early Saturday morning approximately four hours before the game. (Courtesy of Lewis Lazarow.)

The night before the homecoming game, many Alumni Blue Band members take part in the homecoming parade. The parade starts by the Intramural Building and snakes through campus and then up College Avenue to end by the Recreation Building. After walking the parade, the Penn State Alumni Association provides buses for members and takes them back to the Blue Band Building. The parade marchers then enjoy a post-parade reception and pick up their music and charts for practice the next morning. Volunteers and Alumni Blue Band board of director members staff tables to hand out the important information. (Both, courtesy of Lewis Lazarow.)

The Penn State Alumni Association offers buses again the morning of homecoming when Alumni Blue Band members report to the O. Richard Bundy Blue Band Building to pick up instruments or field equipment, charts, music, and breakfast (also donated by the alumni association). The buses take the performers to Holuba Hall, the indoor football practice area. There, the Alumni Blue Band practices for about two hours, listens to announcements, and then walks to the stadium to prepare to march pregame. Within three hours of learning a drill, the band will perform it in front of more than 100,000 spectators. (Both, courtesy of Lewis Lazarow.)

If Penn State has long been known as "Linebacker U" because of the dominant defensive players it has fielded, then it would not be incorrect to suggest it also adopt the name "Twirler U." The Penn State Touch of Blue has been the most dominant majorette line in collegiate twirling over the past two decades, winning 16 national championships in dance twirl and halftime show, most recently in 2019. And the feature twirlers have had similar success in national and world solo twirling championships. Its reputation for excellence has made the Penn State Blue Band's feature twirler position one of the most prestigious and sought-after positions in the nation. Pictured here is the 2002 Touch of Blue majorette squad with feature twirler Bobbie Jo Solomon under the direction of Heather Bean; they won the national collegiate halftime championship. (Courtesy of the Blue Band Office.)

One thing that became very apparent when Penn State joined the Big Ten was that the band programs at other schools had significantly more support than the Blue Band. Many had their own dedicated practice fields and buildings. In 1999, the Blue Band took a very small step in this direction with the acquisition of "the Shack" from the ROTC program. The structure was close to the intramural fields where the band practiced, but was too small to function effectively as both a storage facility for instruments and uniforms and also a place to hold meetings and indoor rehearsals. The band had the Shack until 2004. The university has now repurposed it as the Lion Pantry, assisting students suffering from food insecurity. (Both, courtesy of Stephanie Nimick.)

Without the financial support of the Penn State Alumni Association (PSAA), the dream of a Blue Band Building would never have been realized. Recognizing that it would take the commitment of the entire Penn State family, the PSAA created a special funding campaign: for every two dollars an association member contributed, the association would add an additional dollar. Promoted by a television commercial created by Blue Band alumnus Jeff Hughes, association members responded, and funds were finally acquired to construct a Blue Band Building with sufficient space for all the band's storage, rehearsal, and administrative needs. At the ground-breaking ceremony, the staff of the Blue Band were on hand to shovel the first pails of dirt. From left to right are director O. Richard Bundy, volunteer assistant David Cree, percussion instructor Dave Buzminski, administrative assistant Karen Walk, silk instructor Kathy Smith Bamet, and majorette instructor Heather Bean. (Courtesy of the Blue Band Office.)

The Blue Band Building was completed during the summer of 2004, in time for band camp and the football season. All the instruments and uniforms were moved in before the students arrived on campus. No longer serving any purpose, the trailers were hauled away, but photographs of them were hung in the main rehearsal room as a permanent reminder of the Blue Band's roots. Room 3 in Music Building 1, where the uniforms were stored, was no longer needed either. The director's office was designed with windows looking out across the fields toward Beaver Stadium. (Above, courtesy of Thomas Range II; below, courtesy of Stephanie Nimick.)

Before the construction of the Blue Band Building, all musical practices were held outside. The phrase "It never rains on the Blue Band" meant that even if it was raining (or snowing), members were still expected to come to practice. Very rarely was Blue Band practice cancelled. The new building provided enough space to allow the instrumentalists to actually sit down during rehearsals. Members of the silks and majorettes have their own mirrored practice room so they can practice without having to worry about the weather. (Both, courtesy of the Blue Band Office.)

Traditionally, the Blue Band provided instruments for percussionists as well as sousaphone, mellophone, and baritone players. Those instruments were deemed too expensive for the average student to own. Students in all other instrument sections—trumpets, trombones, saxophones, clarinets, and piccolos—had to provide their own. However, each make and model is slightly different, which meant the Blue Band lacked a truly uniform sound. The only way to solve this problem was to embark on an ambitious campaign: providing band members with matching brass performance instruments. Through support from donors and members of the Floating Lions Club, the Blue Band started to make progress toward this goal. One of the first sections to get new instruments were the trumpets. Also important to note in this photograph is the 2001 uniform update: the hat, which for decades had a plastic silver lyre attached front and center, now had an embroidered PSU monogram. The yarn plume on top, however, remained part of the uniform until 2016. (Courtesy of Jim Lawrence.)

Grateful to everyone who donated funds in support of the Blue Band Building effort, the band paid tribute to their patrons, forming a huge "THANKS" during one of the 2004 halftime shows. Without the support of the membership of the alumni association, the Blue Band would not have a permanent home. (Courtesy of the Blue Band Office.)

Over the next few years, the Blue Band progressively added sections of school-owned instruments. In this photograph from the middle of the pregame fanfare block, the mellophones, baritones, and saxophones are still the old brass versions, while the sousaphones and trumpets are the new matching silver instruments. (Courtesy of Jim Lawrence.)

Feature twirler alumnae Bobbie Jo Solomon (1999–2003) performs with the current feature twirler P.J. Maierhofer (2005–2009) at TailGreat in the Bryce Jordan Center prior to the 2008 homecoming game. These two feature twirlers were the only two in that role during the decade; the 2004 Blue Band had no feature twirler. (Courtesy of Jim Lawrence.)

The Big Ten is home to some of the oldest and most respected collegiate bands, so part of the excitement of being in the Blue Band is traveling to other conference schools to perform for and with their bands. It is a Blue Band bucket list moment to perform the Floating Lions in the only stadium in the western hemisphere larger than Beaver Stadium: "The Big House" at the University of Michigan. (Courtesy of Jim Lawrence.)

Because the Blue Band relies on Penn State Athletics for its travel budget, the number of full-band away game trips varies from year to year. When Pitt was an annual opponent during Penn State's independent years, it was almost a guarantee the band would get two trips in a single season every other year: a trip to Pittsburgh and another trip somewhere in the Northeast. The move to the Big Ten changed all of that. So it was a rare occurrence when the Blue Band made two trips in 2008: north to Ann Arbor for the Michigan game and east to Lincoln Financial Field in Philadelphia for the nonconference game against Temple. Here, director Dr. Bundy stands on the 50-yard-line ladder and conducts the Blue Band's performance of the Penn State alma mater during the pregame show; because of the high number of Penn State alumni in the Philadelphia area, there were plenty of fans wearing blue and white singing along. (Courtesy of the Blue Band Office.)

The year 2008 was a special time for the Penn State Alumni Association. During the annual homecoming ice cream social, the association held a dedication ceremony for the new Alumni Walk outside the Hintz Family Alumni Center. About 30 members of the Alumni Blue Band were on hand to provide music for the occasion. Alumni could purchase and inscribe bricks and pavers to be placed on walkways around the center. (Courtesy of Thomas Range II.)

At the end of the homecoming game, the Blue Band and Alumni Band take the field to play a postgame concert together. Each alum pairs up with a current member to share music in a show that combines traditional Penn State songs, favorites from years past, and selections from the respective homecoming halftime shows. (Courtesy of Thomas Range II.)

At the end of the Floating Lions drill, the Blue Band marches on a drum cadence to create the "Team Aisle" formation. Since the early 1990s, it has been tradition to keep the student section energized and entertained while waiting for the team to emerge from the tunnel by playing a song; initially that was "Rock and Roll" (also known as the "Hey!" song), which since 2012 has evolved into a particularly PSU version of "We Will Rock You." When the team is ready to take the field, the cheerleaders run out holding the huge Penn State flags, leading the team down the aisle to the sideline while the Blue Band plays "The Nittany Lion." Many have noted that unlike most teams, Penn State's home sideline is not under the press box but on the opposite side of the field. This tradition stems from a choice made by former head coach Joe Paterno; fortunately, neither Bill O'Brien nor James Franklin have felt the urge to change it—otherwise the team aisle would have to be completely redrilled! (Courtesy of Jim Lawrence.)

In 2008, the Blue Band instrumentalists' uniform was changed significantly—although to the average Penn Stater, it does not look like anything changed at all. Since there was no need for a convertible concert-to-marching uniform, the old suit-and-trouser combination concept that had been in continuous use since 1963 was discarded, as was the separate plastic overlay. The new uniform preserved the traditional look of the Blue Band while creating something that was far more comfortable and easier to clean. The new "overlay" is actually the uniform's shirt, and is made of cotton. Other than the removal of the shoulder tassels and the addition of blue piping along the edges, it is hard for the untrained eye to distinguish the difference. All of the old uniforms were destroyed to prevent anyone from using one to gain entrance into Beaver Stadium by pretending to be in the band. (Courtesy of the Blue Band Office.)

Some of the most loved and best remembered shows were ones that involved moving parts. The "Rocky" show actually animated two stick-figure boxers to fight each other on the field. Their golden boxing gloves are the bells of the sousaphones. In 2014, another drill capitalized on the popularity of the HBO show *Game of Thrones*, but added a Penn State twist to honor the largest student-run philanthropy in the world: the Penn State Dance Marathon. Called the "Game of THONs," the show played off the allegorical knighthood adventure "The Four Diamonds," the inspiration behind the Four Diamonds Fund to benefit pediatric cancer research. Ultimately, the Knight of the Four Diamonds on the left defeats the evil Pediatric Cancer on the right. (Above, courtesy of the Blue Band Office; below, courtesy of Jim Lawrence.)

Since the acceptance of female instrumentalists in 1973, the Blue Band has come a long way. That first year, there were only five female instrumentalists in the ranks of the band. Today, women usually comprise about 60 percent of the band. According to retired administrative assistant Karen Walk, 66 percent of the lockers in the Blue Band Building are female lockers. (Courtesy of the Blue Band Office.)

Since 2005, upon reaching the end of the homecoming parade route, the alumni mellophones run to the Nittany Lion Shrine for a group photograph. To make the buses back to the Blue Band Building for the post-parade social, the alumni have to rush. Luckily, the parade ends a short distance way. The tradition was started by Barb Garbrick Wolf-Moser, Lew Lazarow, and Jen Warner (Courtesy of Jake Lazarow.)

The Penn State Blue Band was honored in 2005 when it was recognized as one of the best collegiate bands in the nation, receiving the coveted Sudler Trophy. Awarded by the John Philip Sousa Foundation, the purpose of the Sudler Trophy is "to identify and recognize collegiate marching bands of particular excellence that have made outstanding contributions to the American way of life" and is awarded "to a college or university marching band which has demonstrated the highest of musical standards and innovative marching routines and ideas, and which has made important contributions to the advancement of the performance standards of college marching bands over a number of years." The Blue Band is one of only 32 collegiate bands to have received this high honor—but stands in good company alongside nine other Big Ten Conference bands. (Courtesy of Thomas Range II.)

In this image of the Blue Band emerging from the tunnel to form the pregame fanfare block, the band's current seats in the southeast corner of Beaver Stadium are clearly visible. They are in the midst of the student section to keep them energized throughout the game but also positioned in a way that the entire lower deck as well as the north end zone upper deck can hear them. (Courtesy of Jim Lawrence.)

In this photograph of the Blue Band in the stands, note how the sousaphone players create the boundary lines between the band and the student section. The drums are in the middle; above them in order are the mellophones, trumpets, baritones, and trombones. Below are the saxophones, clarinets, and piccolos. The band front is out of frame; they would be sitting below the clarinets at lower left. (Courtesy of the Blue Band Office.)

The tradition of Bandorama was started by Dr. Deihl during the 1978 season. Deihl wanted the Blue Band to perform a revue of the entire season's music in a concert setting. Up until 2018, the performances were in Eisenhower Auditorium; more recently, the concert takes place in the Bryce Jordan Center. Due to the Covid-19 restrictions, there was no Bandorama in 2020. (Courtesy of Jim Lawrence.)

It was not until 2010 that another important piece of Blue Band equipment received a significant upgrade. Made possible by a donation from the Harold Brake family, the scaffolding that the directors had used for decades to oversee practices at the intramural fields was replaced with the Brake Band Tower. The tower allows Blue Band directors a safer way to see how drills look from a fan's point of view. (Courtesy of Jim Lawrence.)

Like many collegiate bands, the Blue Band is "brass heavy," meaning there are significantly more brass instruments than woodwind instruments (clarinets, saxophones, and piccolos). Despite this seeming imbalance, woodwinds are still a vital part of the Blue Band's sound; in fact, having woodwinds gives the Blue Band the opportunity to play music in a way that creates a concert effect even during a field show. Although white gloves are a mandatory part of the uniform, some clarinetists cut the tips off the fingers in order to make playing the instrument a little easier. Because the traditional pregame is the same every week, all Blue Band members memorize the music, which is the reason why these players have empty lyres. The halftime show is a different story, of course, because that show changes every week and the music is not memorized, the only exception being a bowl game show. (Courtesy of Jim Lawrence.)

The Touch of Blue are pictured in their 2010 uniforms during the postgame concert. Many modern collegiate bands—like the Blue Band—are primarily "show bands," working to provide an entertainment experience for fans at football games; thus, there are many more theatrical elements included today than in decades past. It is not unusual for the majorettes and silks to change uniform styles from season to season. (Courtesy of Jim Lawrence.)

The trumpets are the largest section of the Blue Band. Here, ranks J, K, L, and M are in their pregame midfield block positions between the 35- and 45-yard lines. In the background, the crowd is celebrating the Stripe Out, an annual Beaver Stadium tradition since 2015, which looks very impressive from the stands and on the field. (Courtesy of Mark Poblete.)

On September 15, 2012, Penn State opened its season at home against the US Naval Academy—the first time the two teams had played each other since 1974. As the Blue Band finished the national anthem, Beaver Stadium experienced a flyover by two Navy F/A-18s of Strike Fighter Squadron 34. One of the pilots was Blue Band drum line alumnus Lt. Joshua Feldman, who marched from 2002 to 2006. (Courtesy of Jim Lawrence.)

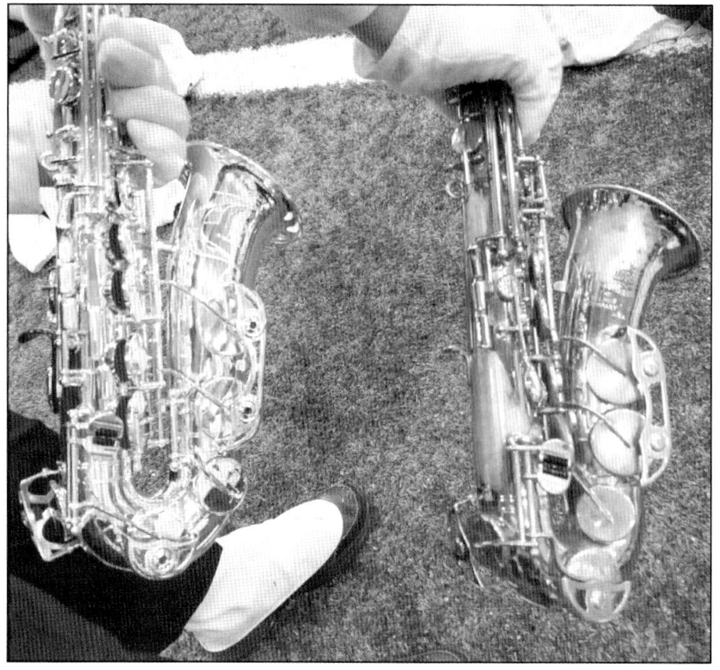

To offer a more uniform sound and look, the Blue Band now has school instruments for all instrumentalists. Students play their personal instruments during practice or use designated school-owned practice instruments. But when there is a performance, the "concert" instruments are taken out. Having the same brand of instrument used by all players offers the consistency of look and sound that major college band programs are always seeking. (Courtesy of Amy Litwiler.)

During a White Out game, the Blue Band seems to almost disappear in a sea of white. The White Out game is declared against the biggest opponent of the season. For almost the past decade, this has been either Michigan or Ohio State. One of the most memorable was the homecoming White Out against Michigan in 2013, which Penn State won 43-40 after four overtimes, the longest game in Big Ten Conference history. This photograph shows a tradition that was only a year old at the time. In the spring of 2012, head coach Bill O'Brien came to the annual Blue Band banquet to request help with starting something new: at the end of every game, win or lose, the Blue Band would lead the entire stadium, including the players and coaches, in singing the alma mater. This tradition continues today. (Courtesy of Jim Lawrence.)

The Blue Band has also performed at professional football games and, in particular, has been a favorite of the Buffalo Bills. The band has been invited to play for their fans four times—in 1989, 1991, 2013, and 2017. For the 2013 trip, the band members practiced and then changed into their uniforms on the practice field before departing. (Courtesy of Jim Lawrence.)

From the end of August to the end of November, hundreds of thousands of loyal Penn Staters roll back into town to cheer the Nittany Lions on to victory. But the Blue Band has some fiercely loyal fans of its own, for whom pregame and halftime is just as important as the final score! (Courtesy of Jim Lawrence.)

There are certain special game-day traditions that Penn State fans do not want to miss, and the Blue Band parade to Beaver Stadium is definitely one of them. Starting from in front of the ORBBBB, the Blue Band marches the one-mile route down University Drive and turns onto Curtin Road to enter the tunnel to line up for its pregame performance. Along the way, band members chant and dance in time with the drum line's "Parade Order" cadence. The entire route is lined with cheering fans, who leave their tailgates to sing and clap along to the school fight songs. (Above, courtesy of Amy Litwiler; below, courtesy of Jim Lawrence.)

The "ALUMS" formation is one of the memorable homecoming traditions for members of the Alumni Blue Band. Close to 400 members of the association, spanning on average 60-plus years of Blue Band history, return to Happy Valley to relive the best part of their college experience. While the Alumni Blue Band performs on the field, the current members of the Blue Band watch from the sideline. (Courtesy of Jim Lawrence.)

In recognition of his impending retirement in May 2015, Penn State honored Dr. Bundy during the 2014 homecoming game against Northwestern, in gratitude for his extraordinary legacy of leadership and service to the decades of students who played in the Blue Band. To show his appreciation, Coach James Franklin invited Dr. Bundy to stand and sing with him and the football team as the Blue Band played the alma mater. (Courtesy of Jim Lawrence.)

Dr. O. Richard Bundy has been the only director in the long history of the Blue Band who was actually a member of the band as an undergraduate student. For the final home show, Blue Band members vote for their favorite numbers from the past season. On November 29, 2014, in honor of Dr. Bundy's final Beaver Stadium appearance as director, the Blue Band members performed a very special favorites show, comprised of three of his arrangements and drill designs: the James Bond medley from the 1983 Sugar Bowl show, "007: A View to a Kill" from 1987, and Chicago's "You're the Inspiration" from 1985. And just like the Blue Band forming the word "HUM" to say goodbye to Hum Fishburn in 1965, the 2014 Blue Band honored Bundy in the same fashion. (Courtesy of Jim Lawrence.)

The Penn State Homecoming Committee has chosen many outstanding Penn State alumni to serve as grand marshal, including football Hall of Fame member Franco Harris, CIA agent Valerie Plame Wilson, and Lara Spencer of ABC's *Good Morning America*. Many are willing to be part of the homecoming entertainment during Alumni Blue Band performances. For homecoming 2015, actor and comedian Keegan-Michael Key served as grand marshal; he was very willing to pose with the Alumni Blue Band at the ice cream social and later borrowed a sousaphone for the homecoming parade. Key received his master's degree in fine arts from the university in 1996. (Above, courtesy of Thomas Range II; left, courtesy of Mark Poblete.)

Since 2010, Knoebel's Park in Elysburg, Pennsylvania, has hosted a Penn State Day, organized by several of the commonwealth campuses. Alumni Blue Band members have been honored to provide the soundtrack for the event, among other pep band opportunities. Unfortunately, the 2020 event was canceled due to Covid-19 concerns. (Courtesy of Thomas Range II.)

After the Blue Band's postgame concert, the drum line forms up to perform its Corner Concert. Originally taking place by the visiting team's tunnel in the northwest corner of Beaver Stadium (hence the name), the percussionists now perform on the 50-yard line. The cymbal section's pushups provide one of the traditional highlights during the performance of "Parade Order." (Courtesy of Lewis Lazarow.)

Depending on how many alumni drum line members from past years attend homecoming and how much practice time they have together over the weekend, they might also perform at the Corner Concert after the homecoming game. The "Parade Order" cadence is heard so often that it is one of the most lasting memories for all band members, but since it has undergone subtle changes over the years, it is always interesting to hear a different version of it from decades past. (Courtesy of Jake Lazarow.)

During the third quarter of every home football game, members of the trumpet section roam Beaver Stadium and play fight songs for the fans. The group will go up an aisle and turn toward the crowd, alternating so both sides of the aisle hear them. (Courtesy of Lewis Lazarow.)

Before stepping off in the Tournament of Roses Parade, the band practices with their uniform tops removed. Since 1989, the "triangle" T-shirt has served as an alternate informal uniform. The white version is worn during Friday afternoon practices to check formations, and either the blue or white version is worn in performance beneath the formal uniform. The tenor drum players are wearing ear protection, which is quite common now among band members. For the parade, the Rose Bowl provided special themed heads for the drum line. The drum heads were not only colorful, but helped promote the event. Unfortunately, the football team lost the game to USC, 52-49. (Both, courtesy of Jake Lazarow.)

The Penn State Nittany Lions have played in the Rose Bowl, "the Granddaddy of Them All," in Pasadena, California, four times. The first was in 1923, but the Blue Band did not make that trip; the band's first bowl game trip was actually to Philadelphia for the Liberty Bowl in 1959. But since then, with the exception of the Aloha Bowl in Hawaii in 1983, the Blue Band has always gone "bowling" with the team, including Penn State's other three Rose Bowl games since becoming a member of the Big Ten Conference, in 1995, 2009, and most recently in 2017. A highlight of the trip is the opportunity to march as part of a 100-plus-year tradition: the 5.5-mile Tournament of Roses Parade down Colorado Boulevard, one of the most watched events across the nation and around the world on New Year's Day. (Courtesy of Jake Lazarow.)

Fans have often wondered what it would be like to sit with the band during a game in Beaver Stadium. The band has a wonderful view of the game—especially during the Stripe Out—but members must also keep their eyes on the drum major to know what and when to play. (Courtesy of Jake Lazarow.)

In 2017, the band traveled to Columbus for the game against Ohio State (OSU). In one of the OSU pregame traditions, the Ohio State Marching Band performs in a concert called the Skull Session, held at St. John Arena four hours before kickoff. The Skull Session is a musical preview for the upcoming game. Visiting bands participate in the session as well. The Blue Band first played the Skull Session in 1993. (Courtesy of Jake Lazarow.)

If a football game is really big, it is slotted to be broadcast nationally in primetime and possibly garners a visit from ESPN's *College GameDay* crew. For the 2017 season, the Penn State–Michigan game was one of the biggest. ESPN's *College GameDay* crew set up its live broadcast on the Old Main lawn, and the Blue Band did its part to contribute to the festivities. (Courtesy of Jake Lazarow.)

As one of its most recognizable symbols, the Blue Band represents Penn State University with pride. The students are not only aware of the legacy they carry, left to them by alumni of decades past, but also that they are responsible for preserving that legacy for the generations to come. Thousands of children watch the Blue Band march and dream of the day they too will proudly wear that uniform. (Courtesy of Jake Lazarow.)

Tallying a 9-2 season in 2017, the Nittany Lions earned their seventh trip to Arizona for the PlayStation Fiesta Bowl, and the Blue Band was right there cheering them on. The band took part in FanFest, one of the many pep rally events leading up to game day, as well as the annual Fiesta Bowl Parade. The band also performed pregame and halftime shows on the field at State Farm Stadium in Glendale, home of the National Football League's Arizona Cardinals. The Lions ended up defeating the Washington Huskies 35-28, remaining undefeated at the Fiesta Bowl. (Both, courtesy of Jake Lazarow.)

One of homecoming's traditions is the ice cream social at the Hintz Family Center, a combined effort between the Penn State Homecoming Committee and the Penn State Alumni Association. Taking place on Friday before the game, both students and alumni enjoy free ice cream, while the Alumni Blue Band provides the entertainment, often with the help of the cheerleaders and the Nittany Lion. Here, alumni percussionist Allen Garbrick performs the popular "cowbell cheer." (Courtesy of Jake Lazarow.)

Because Dr. Bundy was in the Blue Band during his undergraduate years, he decided to actually march in the 2016 homecoming pregame and halftime shows. Each member's block spots are designated a rank letter and a file number; in recognition of his status as a director emeritus, Dr. Bundy's block spot each year in the Alumni Blue Band is "A1." (Courtesy of Lewis Lazarow.)

For pregame, the Blue Band silks now wear a uniform similar to the instrumentalists, harkening back to the silk line's first years in the band. From far away, it is hard to distinguish the difference, but the silk performers are not wearing hats or spats, and the "overlay" is bordered with a row of silver studs. For halftime, a different outfit is often worn to accent the show. Penn State Athletics provides a changing room at Beaver Stadium; however, according to silk instructor Charlie Robey, "When we travel to away games, getting a changing room can be problematic." (Above, courtesy of Jenna Fitzpatrick; below, courtesy of Riley Kelly.)

Penn State played its final scheduled series against traditional rival Pitt—branded the Keystone Classic—between 2016 and 2019. The 2017 contest was held at Beaver Stadium. The Pitt Band made the trip to Happy Valley, and at the end of the game, both bands took the field for the postgame concert. Penn State won 33-17. (Courtesy of Brad Townsend.)

Traditionally, Big Ten teams alternate home games. In 2017, Michigan visited Penn State, so in 2018, Penn State and the Blue Band visited Michigan. Before the game, the Blue Band warmed up on the Michigan Marching Band's practice field. Drum instructor Dave Buzminski is on his way to check on the bass drum players. (Courtesy of Jake Lazarow.)

With the Nittany Lions posting a 9-2 record at the end of the 2018 season, the Blue Band traveled to Orlando, Florida, to support the team and perform at Camping World Stadium during their fourth appearance in the VRBO Citrus Bowl, the seventh-oldest bowl game in the nation. Although the team lost to Kentucky 27-24, the Blue Band had a successful trip, including performances in the annual Citrus Parade down Orange Avenue, at the Penn State pep rally held at Pointe Orlando on New Year's Eve, and parading down Main Street at the Magic Kingdom in Walt Disney World, led by drum major Jack Frisbie. Although just out of view in this image, the Touch of Blue and feature twirler Gillian Brooks twirled special batons with glowing ends, making their routines easier for the crowd to see at night. (Courtesy of Mark Poblete.)

The Covid-19 pandemic has changed the world for everyone, and the Blue Band is no exception. Knowing that the band probably would not be able to perform at any football games in 2020, all returning members were accepted without auditions for only the second time in the band's history. Rookie auditions were still held, and many students attended. Students had to wear masks and be socially distant but still learn the Blue Band's "chair" high step. The chair high step is the signature step the band uses during the traditional pregame show. After learning the step, prospective members must march down the field while playing. (Both, courtesy of Annmarie Mountz.)

Members of the Blue Band and those who were auditioning were given masks specifically made for marching bands, which have a slit by the mouth so students can more safely perform. Not pictured here are the Blue Band bell covers, placed on all the instruments to help prevent the spread of the virus. Even though the band was not allowed to perform during games, a virtual concert was live-streamed over Facebook for parents and fans. It is a true testament to the significance of the Blue Band that despite the challenging conditions, so many students still want to be a part of one of Penn State's greatest traditions. (Both, courtesy of Annmarie Mountz.)

Four

WHERE THEY WORKED, PRACTICED, AND PERFORMED

For the first few years of Penn State's existence, when it was known as the Farmer's High School, the College Building was the only permanent structure on campus. It consisted of dormitories, the library, a cafeteria, classrooms, and a museum as well as an area where a band could practice. Band rehearsals also took place outside—as did the very first seasons of Penn State football, played on the College Building lawn from 1887 to 1892. (Courtesy of Thomas Range II.)

In 1892, a fire destroyed the upper floors of the original College Building. The reconstruction added a bell tower. As more structures were added to campus, the College Building was referred to as the old main building, or Old Main. The Cadet Band continued to practice there, but in 1893, the football team moved to the newly constructed 500-seat Beaver Field, named after James Beaver, former Pennsylvania governor. (Courtesy of Thomas Range II.)

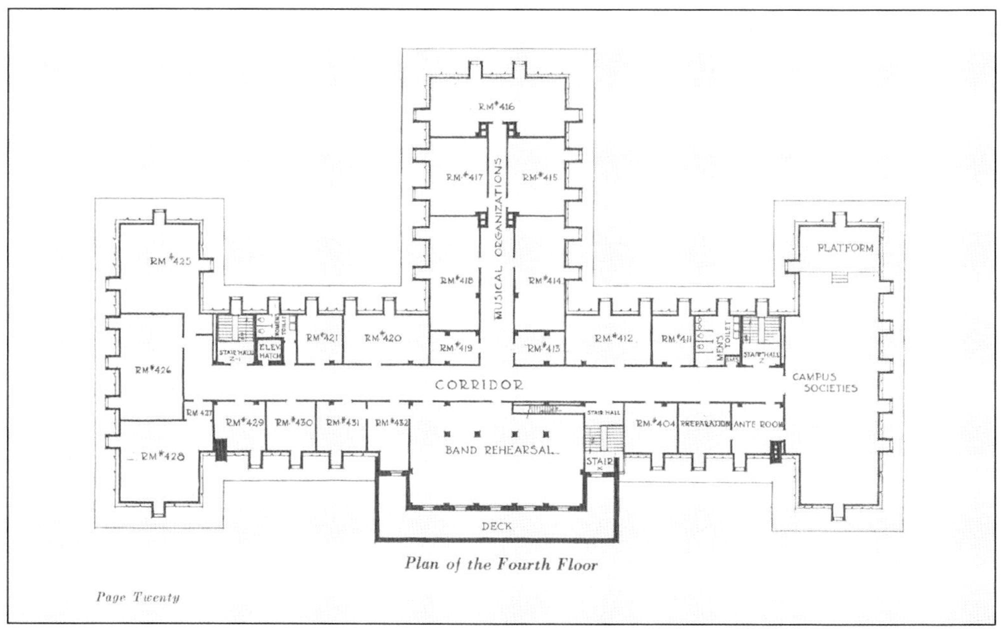

This Old Main floor plan from the 1920s shows a band rehearsal room as well as rooms for musical organizations on the fourth floor. This image was provided by Bryce Mullen, class of 2019 and Blue Band trombone player from 2015 to 2019. (Courtesy of Bryce Mullen.)

In 1909, football games moved from Beaver Field in the middle of campus to New Beaver Field, in the northwest corner of campus. From its initial capacity of 1,200, it expanded to hold a crowd of 30,000 by its final season in 1959. In this image, the Blue Band performs for Dad's Day at New Beaver Field. The baseball grandstand is in the background. (FTPSUPC.)

The Blue Band pregame show of the 1930s was significantly different than the one Penn State fans see today. Back then, the Blue Band would parade around the track that ringed New Beaver Field, playing Penn State fight songs for the crowd before going to the band's seats for the game. The Recreation Building (opened in January 1929 and later known simply as Rec Hall) is in the background. (FTPSUPC.)

Carnegie Library, State College, Pa.

As mentioned previously, Old Main also housed a library. In 1904, the Carnegie Library was built to hold the college's volumes of books. The building served as the campus library until 1940, when Penn State's massive collection outgrew the space, and Pattee Library was built. At this point, Carnegie Library was renamed Carnegie Hall, and the Blue Band's office as well as a practice room were moved there. (Courtesy of Thomas Range II.)

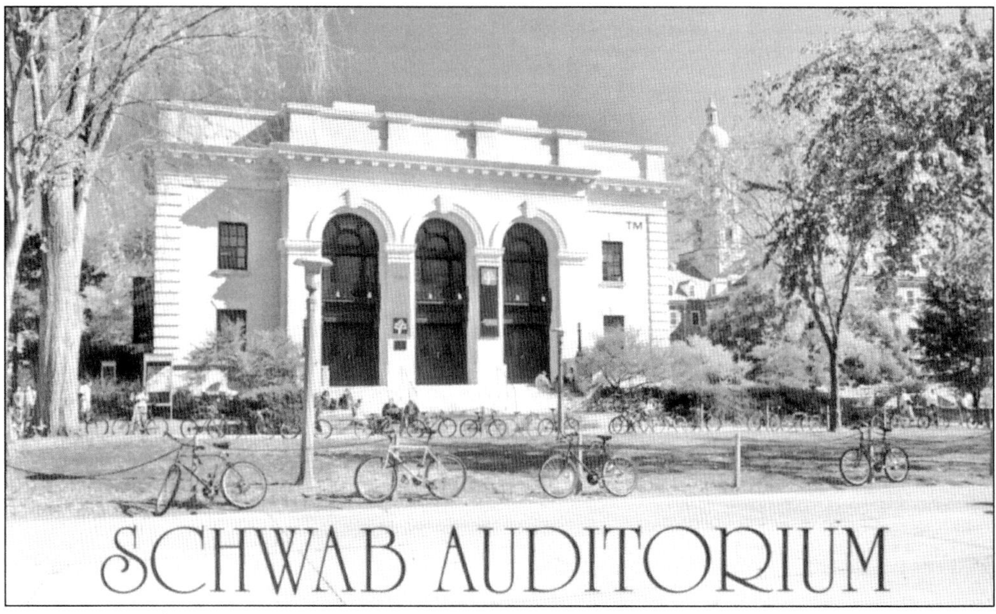

SCHWAB AUDITORIUM

Early Blue Band concerts were played at Schwab Auditorium. Completed in 1903, it was the first campus building financed by a private gift. Charles M. Schwab, founder of Bethlehem Steel and 30-year member of the Penn State board of trustees, gave $150,000 to construct it. The Blue Band has long since expanded beyond the ability to perform at Schwab, but theater productions and small-ensemble concerts still grace its stage today. (Courtesy of Thomas Range II.)

For a brief time, the Armory was the home of the Blue Band. According to Ron Lewis, Blue Band snare drummer from 1963 to 1966, Dr. Dunlop (Blue Band director, 1947–1975) had an office in the Armory. When Dunlop was hired, he created an additional band program—a Concert Blue Band, in which both women and men could participate—that had indoor practices and performed on campus once or twice a semester. This distinguished it from the male-only Marching Blue Band, which performed at football games. Jane Morgan, a Concert Blue Band member from 1961 to 1964, stated that the Concert Blue Band practiced in the Armory for her first two years and then in the Carnegie Building her last two years. The Armory was demolished in January 1964 to make way for expansion of the Willard Building. (Courtesy of Thomas Range II.)

The Chambers Building was completed in 1962 and is the home of the College of Education. Moving the music education faculty to Chambers in 1964 was one of Hum Fishburn's final responsibilities as department chair before his retirement. The Blue Band has long been officially considered a one-credit class within music education; in fact, after making the band, members must still register for it as Music 81. The Blue Band had office space on the second floor until 1994. The Concert Blue Band practiced in Music Building 1; the marching band strictly continued to practice outdoors. However, the Blue Band did have the use of Room 3, in the Music Building 1 basement; this was where all the uniforms were stored, and where at the start of each season, every band member was fitted for their uniform. In this photograph, a young Dr. Deihl and then assistant director O. Richard Bundy can be seen in their cramped Chambers Building office quarters. (Courtesy of Thomas Range II.)

In 1993, Music Building 2 was constructed. The Blue Band offices were moved to the first floor in December 1994, close to the breezeway to Music Building 1. According to Karen Walk, the Blue Band's administrative assistant, the timing was not the best: "They moved us right before the Rose Bowl game. I had no working phone or fax to coordinate travel arrangements for the band!" (Courtesy of Thomas Range II.)

The Blue Band has never had its own dedicated practice field. Throughout the 1970s and into the early 1980s, the Blue Band practiced in a parking lot where the Katz Building stands today. According to Blue Band alumnae Kathi Anderson, "Shin splints were common." As a rookie in 1975, Cathy Bronsdon stated she had to march her first game with swollen legs as a result of these practice conditions. (FTPSUPC.)

In 1978, Blue Band director Ned C. Deihl created the concept of Bandorama. Near the end of the season, the Marching Blue Band performed an indoor concert review of the halftime music. The performances were held in Eisenhower Auditorium until 2018. Initially named University Auditorium when it was opened in 1974, the venue was renamed in honor of Milton S. Eisenhower, who served as university president from 1950 to 1956. (Courtesy of Thomas Range II.)

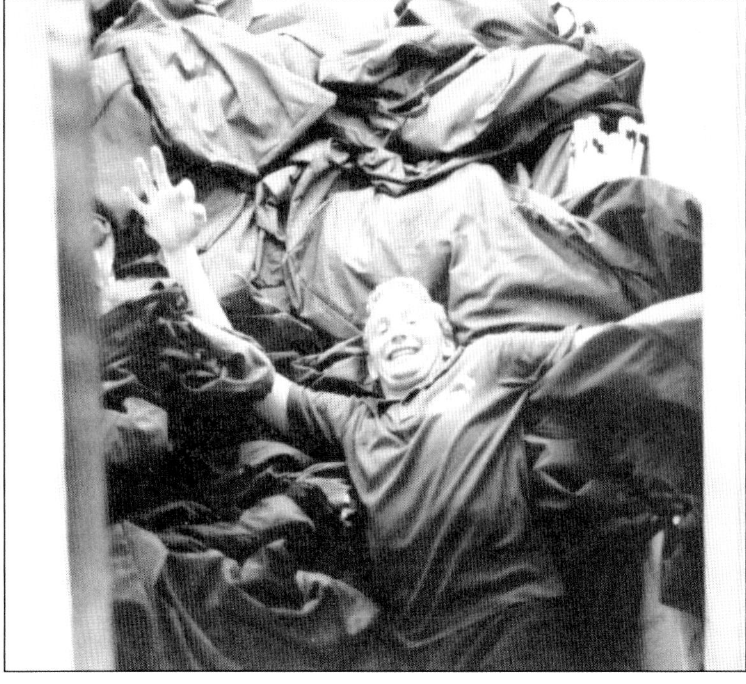

The Blue Band managers required the use of an elevator to move the hundreds of garment bags filled with uniforms down to the basement of Music Building 1. In this photograph, Blue Band manager Joel Thomas tries not to be overwhelmed as the elevator door closes. Uniforms were stored in Room 3 until the completion of the Blue Band Building in 2004. (Courtesy of Thomas Range II.)

From the 1980s to the present day, the Marching Blue Band has practiced on the intramural field at the corner of University Drive and Services Road on Mondays, Wednesdays, and Fridays. This location is one of the farthest corners of campus, but being directly across from East Halls means that all the freshmen living there receive an early-morning game day wakeup call, courtesy of the Blue Band. Tuesday night rehearsals have been held at various locations around the campus over the years. During the 1980s and 1990s, Tuesday night practices were held on a field near the golf course across Atherton Street from Rec Hall. More recently, the band has practiced on the indoor football practice field at Holuba Hall. A permanent, dedicated Blue Band practice field, located behind the O. Richard Bundy Blue Band Building, has been a subject of discussion. (Courtesy of Thomas Range II.)

To keep the school-owned instruments—percussion, sousaphones, baritones, and mellophones—conveniently close for practices, the band purchased a truck trailer for storage in the early 1970s and parked it at the intramural field. That trailer was also used for sports camps during summers. As the band membership expanded, a second trailer was added in 1986, connected by a raised wooden dock. Throughout these years, the trailers served multiple purposes: equipment storage, dressing room, bulletin board, rain shelter, meeting location, and dining room, among others. Pictured here are the Blue Band officers who painted the letters on the second trailer in 1987. Treasurer Mark Sperry (third from left in back) did the lettering layout. These trailers remained a visible fixture at the intramural practice field until the completion of the Blue Band Building in 2004; a photograph of them hangs on the wall of the main rehearsal room as a perpetual reminder of how far the band has come. (Courtesy of Thomas Range II.)

The Bryce Jordan Center is not only the current location of the Bandorama concert, but was also home to a tradition called TailGreat from 1997 until 2013. The Bryce Jordan Center opened three hours ahead of kickoff, with the Blue Band as the main entertainment. The band performed traditional fight songs as well as the halftime music for the upcoming show. (Courtesy of Thomas Range II.)

As the trailers were getting older and Blue Band membership was increasing, a more permanent building was needed to store instruments. "The Shack," previously used for years by the Penn State ROTC, became available in 1999. Just a short distance from the intramural practice field the band uses, it only had enough room for school instruments and a few supplies. Here, students line up outside to receive instruments and music. (Courtesy of Stephanie Nimick.)

After joining the Big Ten and seeing what facilities other comparable schools had for their marching band programs, Penn State, with great support from the Penn State Alumni Association, finally acquired the funds needed to construct a permanent home for the Blue Band. The building has practice rooms for the band and band front, staff offices, a music library, an archive room, equipment room, uniform storage room, male and female locker rooms, and restrooms. It was completed in August 2004, with a formal dedication ceremony on October 24. During homecoming weekend in October 2015, in honor of Bundy's retirement as Blue Band director and with appreciation for all his hard work and dedication, the structure was officially renamed the O. Richard Bundy Blue Band Building (ORBBBB). (Courtesy of Thomas Range II.)

For a short time, after completing the homecoming parade, the Alumni Blue Band met for a social at the Nittany Lion Inn, an event that was the brainchild of Blue Band majorette alumnae Abby Diehl. Much of the practice time on Saturday mornings was devoted to catching up with fellow alums; having a post-parade social shifted that catch-up time, so Saturday could be devoted to practice for the day's performances. Alumni Blue Band Association board meetings were also held at the inn. Once the ORBBBB was completed, these events were moved there. The Penn State Alumni Association has generously provided bus transportation for the Alumni Blue Band members from the end of the two-mile homecoming parade route at the Lion Shrine back to the building, thus preventing a two-mile parade from turning into a 3.5-mile round trip. (Courtesy of Thomas Range II.)

Probably the most well-known and beloved venue in which the Blue Band plays is Beaver Stadium. At the end of the 1959 season, New Beaver Field was disassembled into 750 separate pieces, which were then trucked the 1.5 miles down Park Avenue and reconstructed in the stadium's present location in time for the start of the 1960 season. From its initial seating capacity of 46,284, Beaver Stadium is now the second-largest in the western hemisphere, behind only Michigan Stadium, home of the University of Michigan Wolverines. The band usually plays for all home games to a crowd of 106,572, although seating capacity has been exceeded 14 times since 2007, with the largest-ever crowd of 110,889 in attendance for the game against Ohio State in 2018. Unfortunately, due to the Covid-19 pandemic, the Blue Band was not able to attend any football games in the 2020 season. (Courtesy of Thomas Range II.)

Five

Some Blue Band Notables

George Deike is credited with founding the Cadet Band and starting Blue Band history, although music was not his career. Graduating in 1903 as a mining engineer, Deike founded the Mine Safety Appliance Company. He served as president of the alumni association and the board of trustees. The Deike Building, home of the College of Earth and Mineral Sciences on the University Park campus, is named after him. (FTPSUPC.)

Wilfred Otto "Tommy" Thompson was the first professional director of the Cadet Band. He was hired in 1914 as the third member of the music faculty, and under his guidance, the band evolved in numerous ways. During World War I, he changed the name of the band to the College Military Band, and then in 1923, he created the name "Blue Band." As both a professor and performer, he was cognizant of the changing interests of his students and their audience, setting aside his personal distaste for modern forms of popular music to expand the band's repertoire. After James Leyden initially composed the music and lyrics to "The Nittany Lion," Thompson and Hummel Fishburn worked with him to polish it; it has been a beloved school song for almost 100 years. By the time he retired after 25 years, the band had grown from a student-run organization of 25 to a professionally run 150-member band. (Courtesy of Blue Band Office.)

Hummel Fishburn, or "Hum," was the second director of the Blue Band. Working with Tommy Thompson during his Penn State undergraduate career, they founded the Alpha Zeta chapter of Phi Mu Alpha, the professional music fraternity. As a faculty member, he inherited a purely military band and slowly converted it into a collegiate band. He became head of both the Departments of Music and Music Education at Penn State. All three of his sons became Blue Band members. Though he gave up the directorship of the Blue Band to James Dunlop in 1947, Fishburn continued to be involved, writing drill for the shows until 1962 and announcing for the band's performances at games up until his death in 1976. Among the innovations he introduced to the Blue Band were playing student-composed music during football game performances and increasing the performance marching speed from 120 to 180 beats per minute, making it one of the fastest marching bands in the nation. (Courtesy of Blue Band Office.)

Sisters Edith and Edna Murray were two of the first women in the Blue Band. Neither had any intention of joining a marching band, but when they auditioned for the concert band and the orchestra in 1944, Hum Fishburn asked them if they wanted to be in the Blue Band. The United States was fighting in World War II; most able-bodied men were in the military overseas, and there was a shortage of musicians. Willing to play in any band, the sisters said yes. Edith played flute in the Blue Band. Edna played oboe, but since that was not a marching band instrument, she played cymbals instead. At homecoming in 2007, both sisters were honored by the Penn State Alumni Association. Edith's flute instructor when she was younger was none other than James Dunlop. (Both, courtesy of Edith Murray.)

James Dunlop, an associate professor of music, was hired by Hum Fishburn in 1947 to be director of the Blue Band. Dunlop was the third paid director in Blue Band history. Standing six foot, four inches tall, he was a commanding presence. He was also a stickler for punctuality and perfection. He was known to leave students behind on trips—and at one point, when Dunlop himself was running late, actually scolded the bus driver for waiting for him. Under his leadership, the Blue Band continued to grow in size, but Dunlop was also known for limiting the growth of the band in order to preserve what he felt was the proper balance of instrumentation. He established traditions like high school Band Day and the Alumni Blue Band. (Courtesy of Blue Band Office.)

Jeff Robertson is credited with the creation of the drum major flip in 1971. Before the flip, the drum major usually twirled the baton or did a trick of some sort with the mace. Robertson was an acrobat and decided on a back flip. A few years later, drum major Ron Louder changed it to a front flip, which became the established drum major tradition to this day. (Courtesy of Blue Band Office.)

Judy Shearer (later Lawrence) was the first majorette for the Blue Band. In January 1972, she convinced Dr. Dunlop to watch her twirl in the hopes of being in the Blue Band. Dunlop was so impressed by her audition, he agreed to add a squad of 12 majorettes, making them the first females in the Blue Band since World War II. (Courtesy of Blue Band Office.)

Lori Donaldson (1974–1978) was the first majorette named as the feature twirler, although she was never given a title. She did not have a special outfit completed in time for her first game, so she used an old high school competition outfit that was a different shade of blue. As luck would have it, someone took a picture, which ended up on the cover of a Beaver Stadium pictorial that season. (Courtesy of Blue Band Office.)

In 1974, after watching the Blue Band flag corps perform at halftime, Colleen Schaeffer Rickenbacher made an offhand comment to Dr. Dunlop, stating that she could do a better job with the flags. Dunlop turned to her and said, "Fine, then do it." Over the next five years, she turned the flag corps into a silk squad that did routines as true visual accompaniment to the band. (Courtesy of Blue Band Office.)

Ned C. Deihl became director of the Blue Band unexpectedly in 1975 when James Dunlop passed away. Deihl proved that he was more than ready for the position since he had been assistant director since 1962. His biggest contribution was the Floating Lions drill, which he wrote in 1965 and which is still used today, although it has been tweaked to accommodate more performers. In 1978, Deihl created Bandorama, a concert-hall performance of the season's halftime music. He inherited a band with about 166 members; by the time he retired in 1996, he had grown the band to 275. Deihl changed the band's marching style to be more in line with Big Ten schools and is also credited with making marching part of the Blue Band audition process. (Courtesy of Blue Band Office.)

Lori Bowers was the second person to hold the title of feature twirler but was the first to be known as the Blue Sapphire. Bowers was at first called the Star Sapphire, but since sapphires came in many colors, it was decided to change the name to Blue Sapphire. She was the feature twirler for the Blue Band for the 1978–1981 seasons and notably survived her first bowl trip to Louisiana for the Sugar Bowl against Alabama on January 1, 1979, not realizing until returning home that she had mononucleosis. She met her future husband, Dave Uhazie, in the band. He played trumpet and was band president in 1981. Both of their children, Doug and Patrick, were in the Blue Band as well. In 2005, Lori and Dave created the Lori Bowers and Dave Uhazie Endowed Feature Twirler Scholarship Fund. (Courtesy of Blue Band Office.)

Sue Delanko was a Blue Band majorette from 1980 to 1984. After graduating, she joined the Blue Band staff as majorette coordinator for the Touch of Blue. She held the position from 1984 to 1993. Through her tenure as twirler and coordinator, she was a part of three national championship games but always felt she left the program one year too early, just missing that first Rose Bowl trip. (Courtesy of the Blue Band Office.)

Kathy Smith Bamet joined the Blue Band staff as silk coordinator in 1982. Her first bowl trip was the national championship game at the Sugar Bowl that year. She held the position until 2019. During her tenure as silk instructor, the squad performed increasingly intricate and entertaining drills. (Courtesy of Blue Band Office.)

Charlie Robey was a member of the silk line during the 1976 and 1977 seasons. During the late 1980s, Kathy Smith Bamet asked Robey for help with the squad, and he became a volunteer. During the 1990s, Robey became the assistant silk instructor and started to create some drills. Upon Bamet's retirement in 2019, he was elevated to silk instructor. (Courtesy of Blue Band Office.)

Of all the current Blue Band staff, percussion instructor Dr. David Buzminski has been with the Blue Band the longest. Hired in 1983, "Buzz" has trained hundreds of Blue Band percussionists. A talented arranger as well, Buzminski has had many of his percussion arrangements published. (Courtesy of Blue Band Office.)

Greg Stock became a part-time drum major in 1982 after the current drum major, Tony Petroy, broke bones in both his hands after an awkward landing while practicing the flip. Stock was a freshman at the time and filled in for the drum major's pregame flip responsibility, while Petroy did the conducting in the stands. After Petroy graduated, Stock became the sole drum major for the next four years. However, he suffered a serious injury of his own, fracturing his ankle during drum major auditions in 1983. Fortunately, it healed in time for the season, and he did not miss a performance. Stock is still the longest-serving drum major in Blue Band history, having performed his duties for five seasons. In 1997, Stock created the Stock Family Drum Major Endowment Fund, which provides scholarships for the Blue Band drum major position. (Courtesy of Kris [Dottie] Kokosko.)

Brad Townsend is currently the director of the University of Pittsburgh Marching Band; however, he started his collegiate marching band career at Penn State. Townsend was a sousaphonist in the Blue Band from 1980 to 1984 and served as president of the band his senior year. He attended the University of Illinois at Urbana-Champaign for his master's degree, then returned to the Blue Band in 1988 as a graduate assistant for the next three years. After graduating with his doctorate, Townsend became director of bands for Temple (1998–2002), Oregon State (2002–2013) and then the University of Pittsburgh (2013 to present). Townsend still plays sousaphone, and when his schedule at Pitt allows it, he returns to perform with the Alumni Blue Band at homecoming. He has also guest conducted the Blue Band when the Pitt Band visited Beaver Stadium. (Courtesy of Brad Townsend.)

John Mitchell was the first black and first male feature twirler at Penn State. Sharing the feature twirler position with Lori Branley for the 1989, 1990, and 1991 seasons, Mitchell was the lone feature twirler in 1992. Originally, he was at the University of Pittsburgh, but when Pitt refused to allow him to twirl, instead offering him a position on the silk line, he transferred to Penn State and auditioned for the Blue Band. Mitchell has won collegiate championship and world open twirling titles. After graduation, Mitchell was a competitor on the television show *America's Got Talent*, and though he was eliminated from competition, he garnered rave reviews. He also made other television and film appearances, including *Showtime at the Apollo*; served as an international judge with the National Baton Twirling Association; and coached numerous national twirling champions. (Courtesy of Blue Band Office.)

Karen Walk was the Blue Band's administrative assistant for 27 years. Hired in 1987, she attended numerous bowl trips, coordinated countless performances, and helped get the band into the new Blue Band Building. She retired in June 2013 but still keeps in touch with many Blue Band alumni throughout the country. (Courtesy of Karen Walk.)

On September 8, 1990, Mike "Bull" Harrell took the field as the first African-American drum major in Blue Band history. He started his Blue Band career on baritone, then auditioned for and was selected as drum major on the basis of "his outstanding leadership skills, athletic ability, and musical talent," as director Ned C. Deihl put it. Harrell served as drum major for the 1990 and 1991 seasons. (Courtesy of Blue Band Office.)

Heather Bean joined the staff of the Blue Band in 1994 as majorette instructor. Under her guidance, the Touch of Blue has won multiple collegiate halftime championships and dance twirl championships. As well as being the majorette instructor, Bean also works part-time in the Blue Band Office. (Courtesy of Blue Band Office.)

The Blue Band is very dependent on volunteers. One of the most loyal and hardest working has been Dave Cree. Cree joined the staff in 1996 and assists the band in instrument repairs. He also assists the managers and helps with attendance and medical concerns. The year 2020 was his 25th year with the Blue Band. (Courtesy of Blue Band Office.)

O. Richard "Dick" Bundy has been the only Blue Band director that was actually a member of the Blue Band. After graduating in 1970, Bundy enlisted in the Army for three years and was part of the 50th Continental Army Command Band in Virginia. He used funds from the GI Bill to go to the University of Michigan. A graduate position opened up with the Blue Band in 1980, and Bundy came to Penn State to pursue his doctorate. In 1983, he became the assistant director of the band; in 1988, he earned his doctorate; and in 1996, he became director of athletic bands and, more specifically, the Blue Band. He retired in 2015, and the Blue Band Building was renamed in his honor. (Courtesy of the Blue Band Office.)

Dean Otthofer Devore was a trumpet player in the Blue Band from 1984 to 1988. He started to serve as the Blue Band announcer in 1994 at away games and bowl trips. In 1995, he also became the announcer for TailGreat. In 2000, Devore became the Beaver Stadium football announcer, and in 2005, he also announced for the Blue Band at home and away games. (Courtesy of John Balogh.)

P.J. Maierhofer Burkin was the Blue Sapphire feature twirler from 2005 to 2010. She was the first recipient of the Lori Bowers and Dave Uhazi Endowed Feature Twirler Scholarship. After graduating, Burkin started the Blue Sapphire Classic, a twirling competition held at Rec Hall. Over its six years of existence, she raised almost $100,000 for the scholarship fund. (Courtesy of Blue Band Office.)

Greg Drane is the sixth director of the Blue Band. He earned dual undergraduate degrees in music education and saxophone performance from Bethune-Cookman University. Drane started his Blue Band career as a graduate assistant in 2002 while working on his master's degree in music education. In 2005, he became the assistant director, responsible for directing the athletic pep bands, including the Pride of the Lions basketball bands and the Power Players hockey band; during this time, he started the Fall Athletic Band for the women's volleyball games. He held the assistant director position until Dr. Bundy's retirement in 2015. Drane has designed and arranged some of the most recent highly popular halftime shows such as the "Moving Picture Show" and "Game of THONs." He successfully defended his doctoral dissertation in 2020, *An Oral History of the Navy Band B-1: The First All-Black Navy Band of World War II*. Dr. Bundy served as his advisor. (Courtesy of Annmarie Mountz.)

Matt Freeman was the Blue Band's second male feature twirler, holding the position from 2010 to 2014. During his tenure, he won multiple collegiate twirling competitions, including six NBTA world championships. He is married to Meredith Semion Freeman, former Penn State majorette captain; together, they coach the M Twirling Team. In 2017, he returned to the Blue Band as the feature twirler coach. (Courtesy of Blue Band Office.)

During homecoming in 2016, drum major Jimmie Frisbie was selected as homecoming king. Frisbie comes from a long Blue Band lineage. Both of his parents, Dan (saxophone) and Ann Spinelli Frisbie (clarinet), his uncle Mike and his grandfather Floyd (both sousaphones), and his brother Jack (trombone) were all in the Blue Band. Jimmie is a trumpet player. (Courtesy of Jake Lazarow.)

Wanda Hockenberry joined the Blue Band staff in May 2017 as the administrative assistant. Hockenberry came from Penn State's Human Resources Development Center. Using her organizational skills and her approachable personality, she has quickly become an integral part of the Blue Band family. (Courtesy of Blue Band Office.)

Alto saxophone player Katie Schreckengast was a member of the Blue Band when she won the title of Miss Pennsylvania in 2017. For the talent segment of the competition, she played Beyonce's "Listen" on her saxophone. Schreckengast also received a $7,000 scholarship from the pageant and has returned to Penn State often. (Courtesy of Annmarie Mountz.)

MADE IN THE
USA